Philippe Corentin

STUPID QUESTIONS

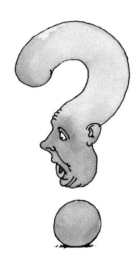

FIREFLY BOOKS

A Firefly Book

Published by Firefly Books Ltd. 2018

Original Title: *Questions Idiotes*
Original French language copyright © 2017 *l'école des loisirs*, Paris
This English translation copyright © 2018 Firefly Books

First printing

Library and Archives Canada Cataloguing in Publication

Corentin, Philippe
[Questions idiotes. English]
     Stupid questions / Philippe Corentin.
Translation of: Questions idiotes.
ISBN 978-0-228-10132-1 (hardcover)
     1. Parent and child–Humor. I. Title. II.Title: Questions
idiotes. English
PN6231.P2C6713 2018   306.87402'07   C2018-901141-6

Published in the United States by   Published in Canada by
Firefly Books (U.S.) Inc.   Firefly Books Ltd.
P.O. Box 1338, Ellicott Station   50 Staples Avenue, Unit 1
Buffalo, New York 14205   Richmond Hill, Ontario L4B 0A7

Text and illustrations by Philippe Corentin
Translator: Flash Rosebury

Printed in China

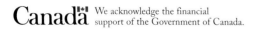

Canada We acknowledge the financial
support of the Government of Canada.

To Elsa?

4

7

12

14